BLOOD OF JESUS

Copyright © 2025 by Undrey Nicholson
eBook   : 978-1-966954-20-0
Hardback : 978-1-966954-18-7
Paperback: 978-1-966954-19-4
LCCN   : 2 0 2 5 9 0 6 9 2 4

Printed in the United States of America.

2

3

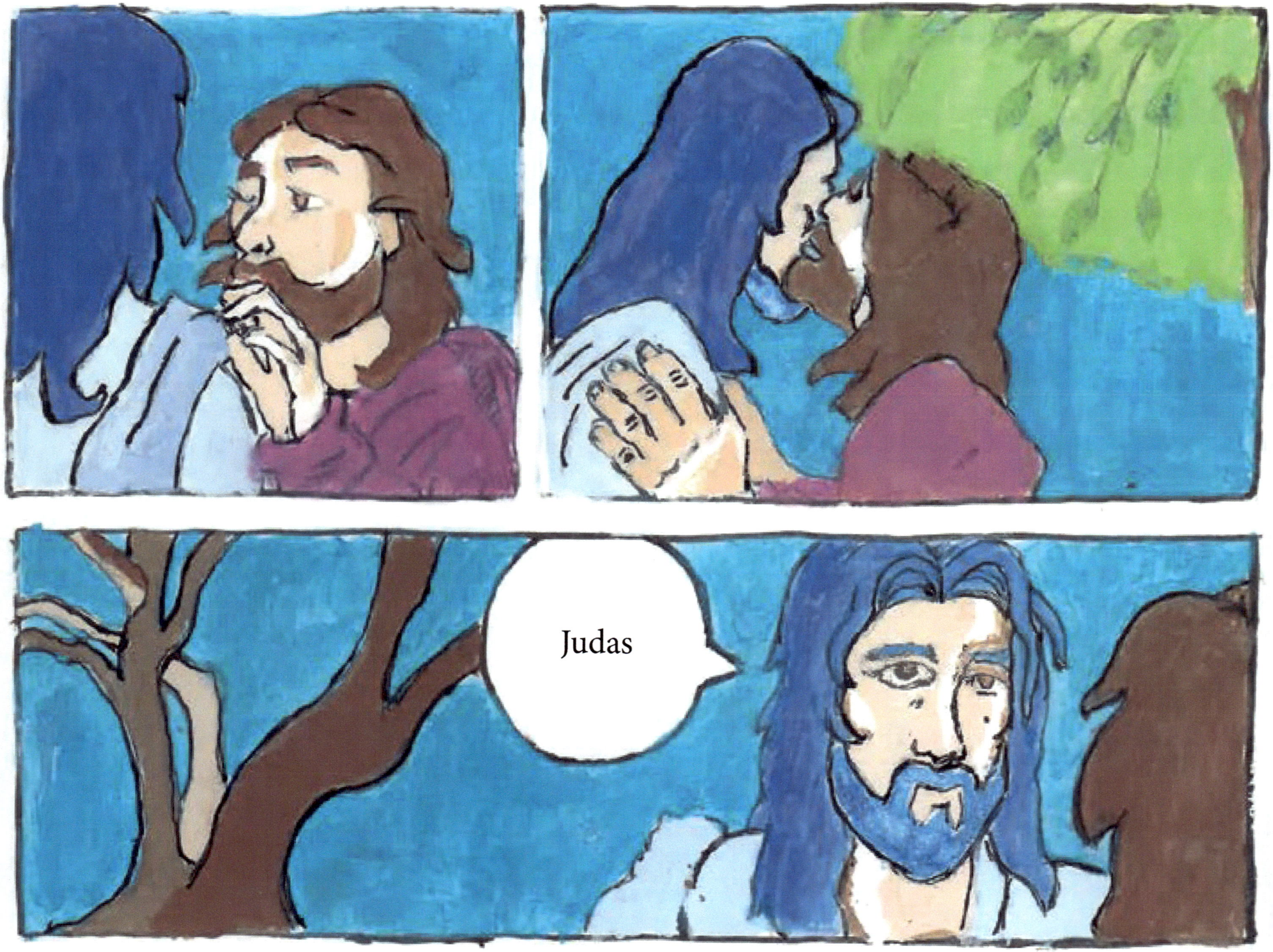
Judas

5

6

7

Jesus knelt down to the man...
My ear...
Peter put the knife down.
Jesus picked up the ear and put it back on...

9

A criminal brought in for questioning. That's all. He broke the temple laws.

Blasphemy!

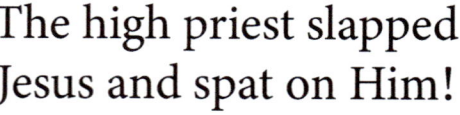

The high priest slapped
Jesus and spat on Him!

The high priest...
wanted Jesus to die...

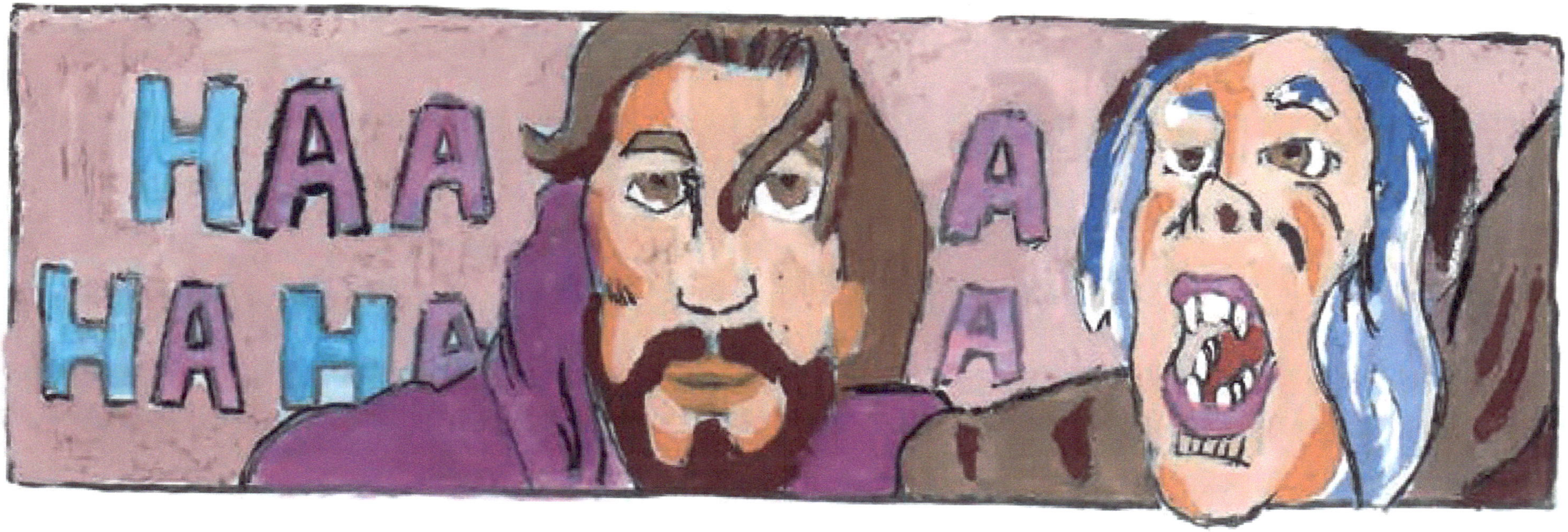
HAA
HAHA
A
A

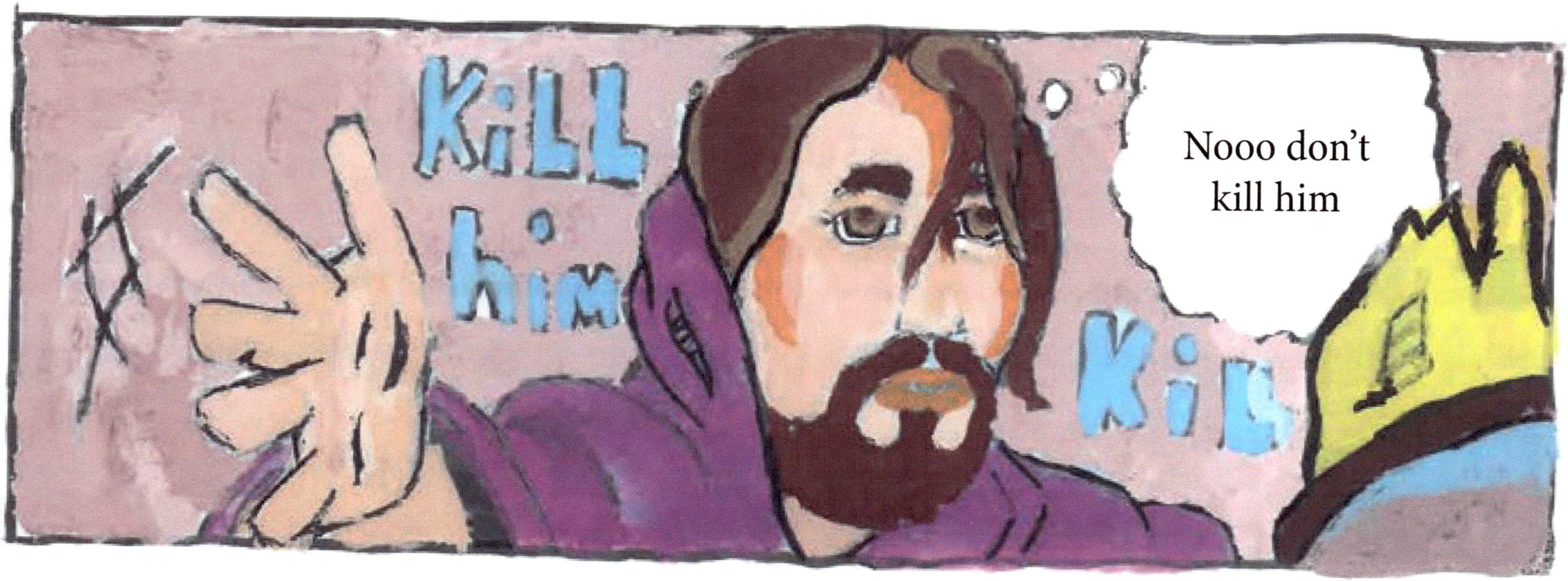
KiLL
him
Nooo don't kill him
KiL

15

16

Here's your money back! Take it...

No! That's yours.

I've sinned. I betrayed an innocent man!

17

Now go...

Please

18

20

It was looking like... hours going by fast in the desert.

Judas ran in to the desert because he denied Jesus...

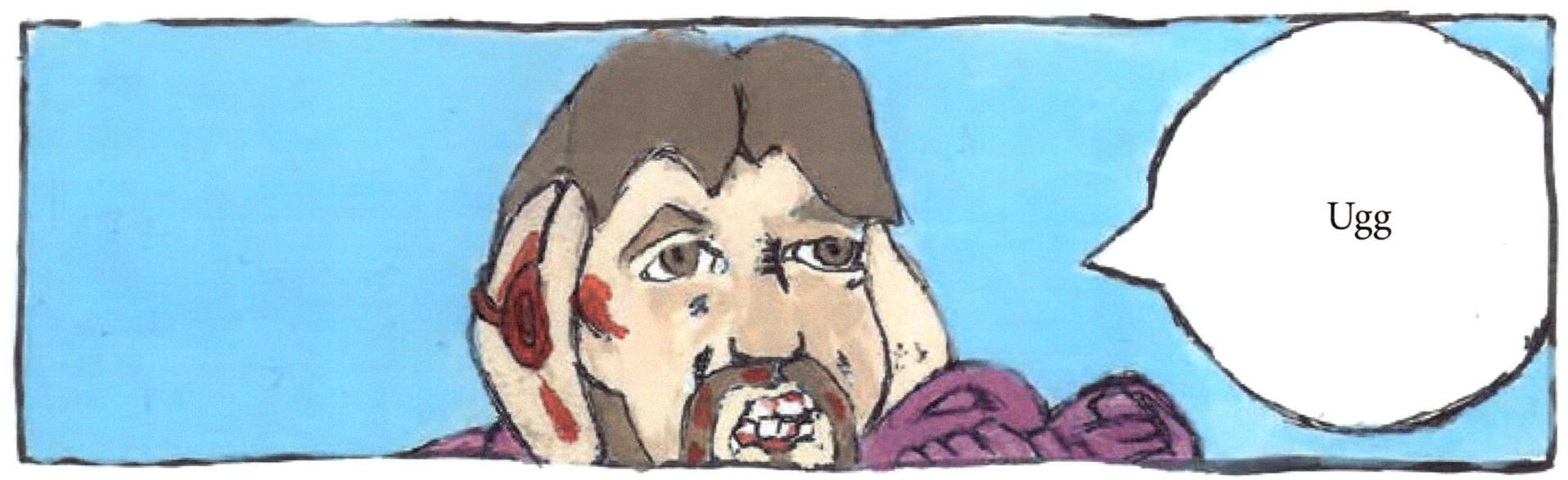

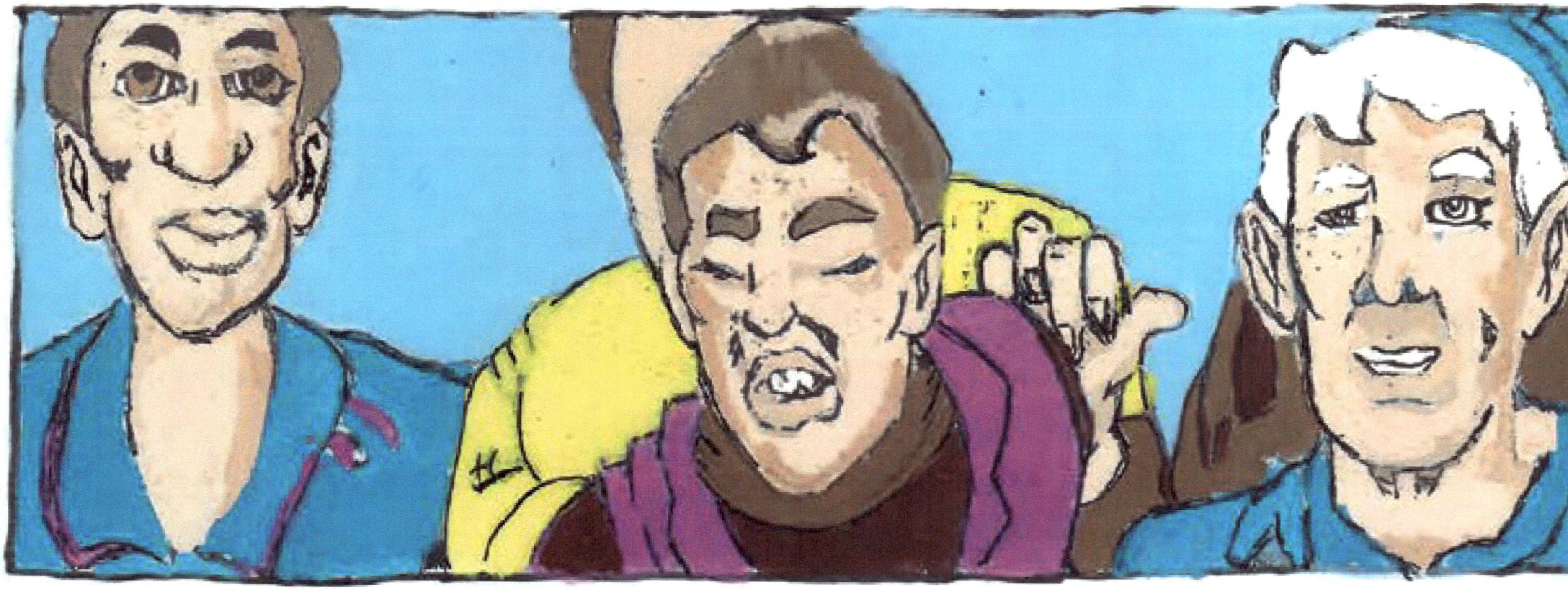

He tied a rope around the tree... to hang himself...

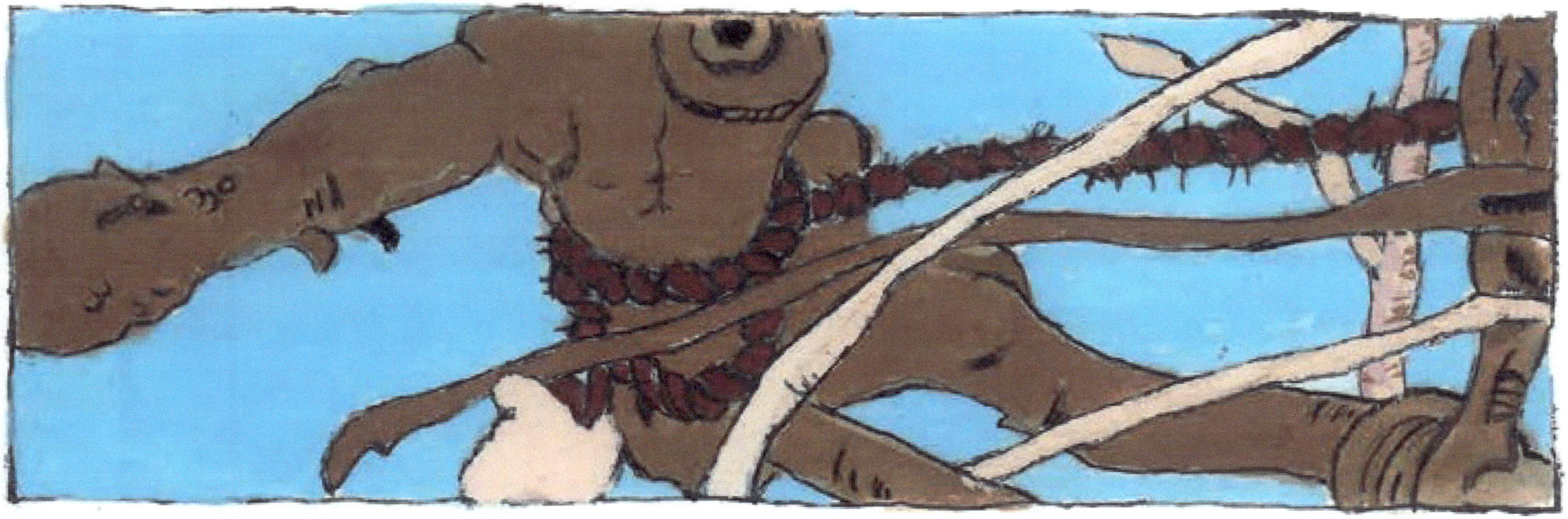

28

31

Free him

Barabbas stuck his tongue at the Romans

Barabbas walked down the stairs... and threw out the crowd of people...

What would you have me...
do with Jesus the Nazarene?

Have him crucified!

36

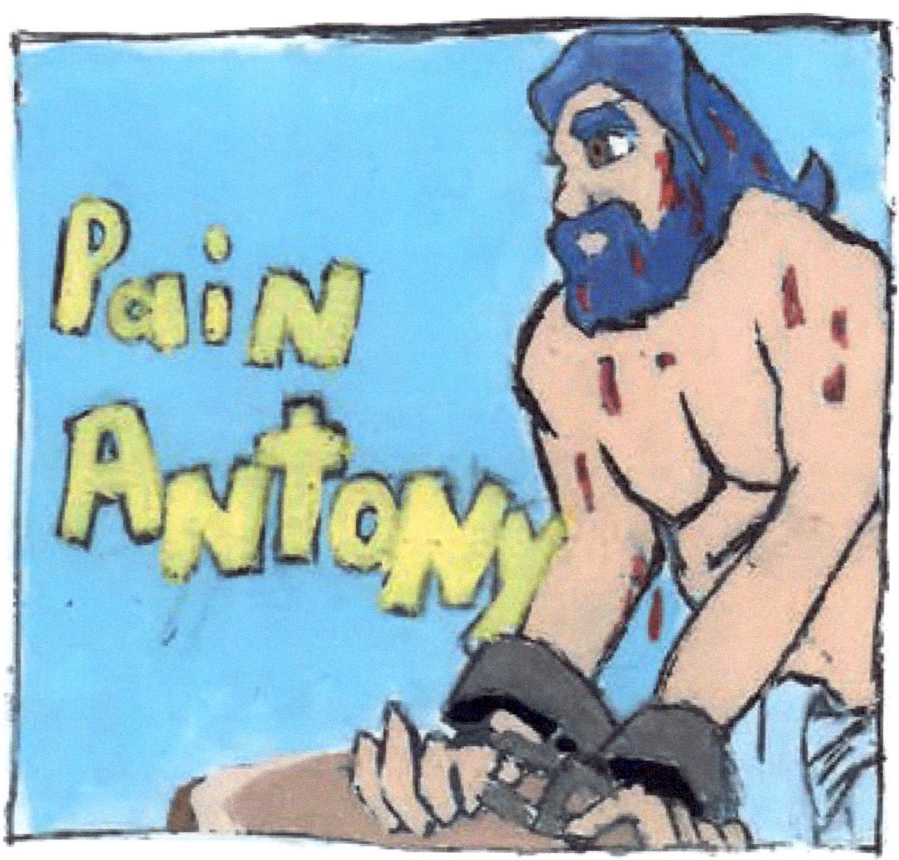

Go and start now...

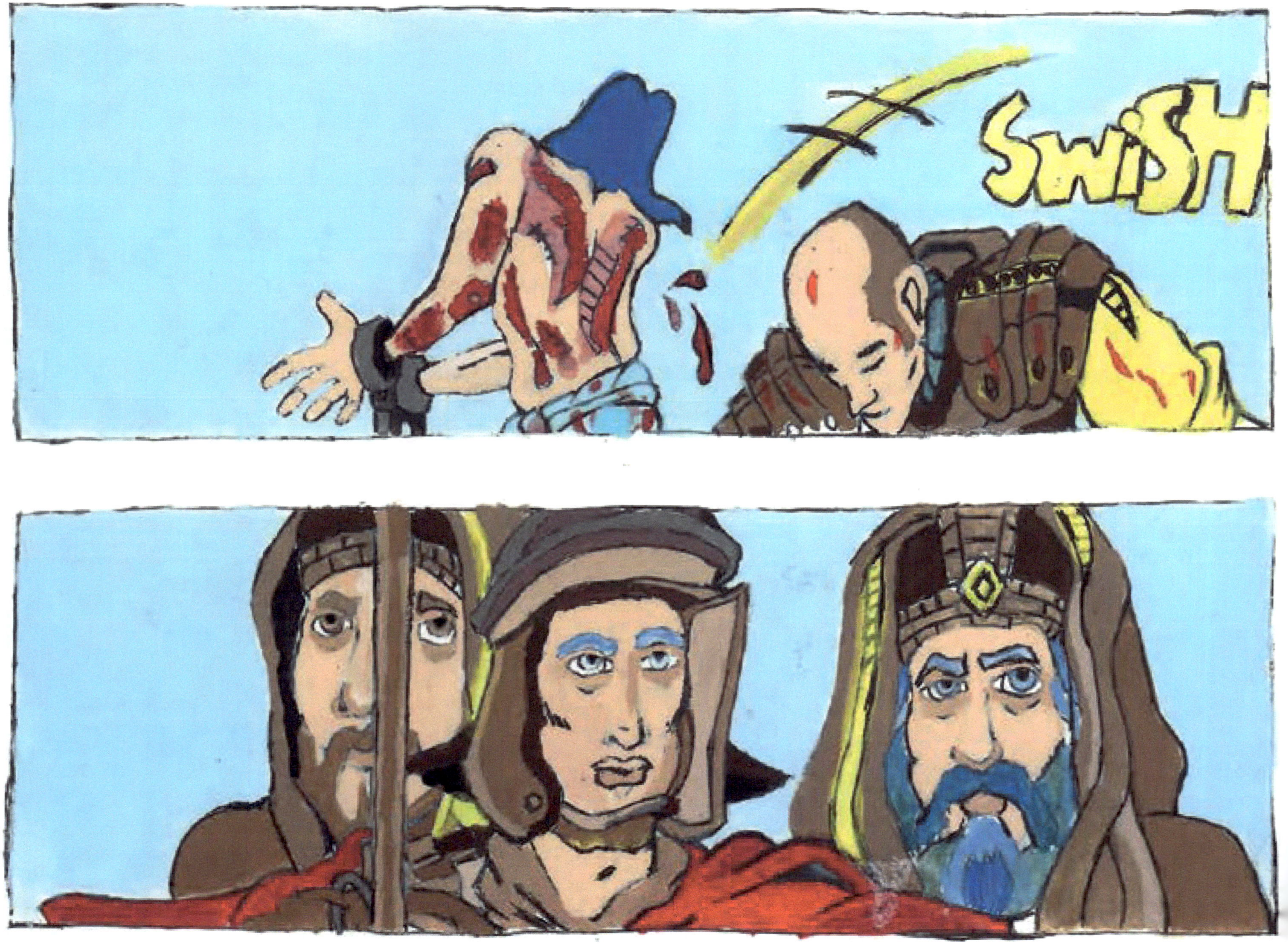
SWiSH

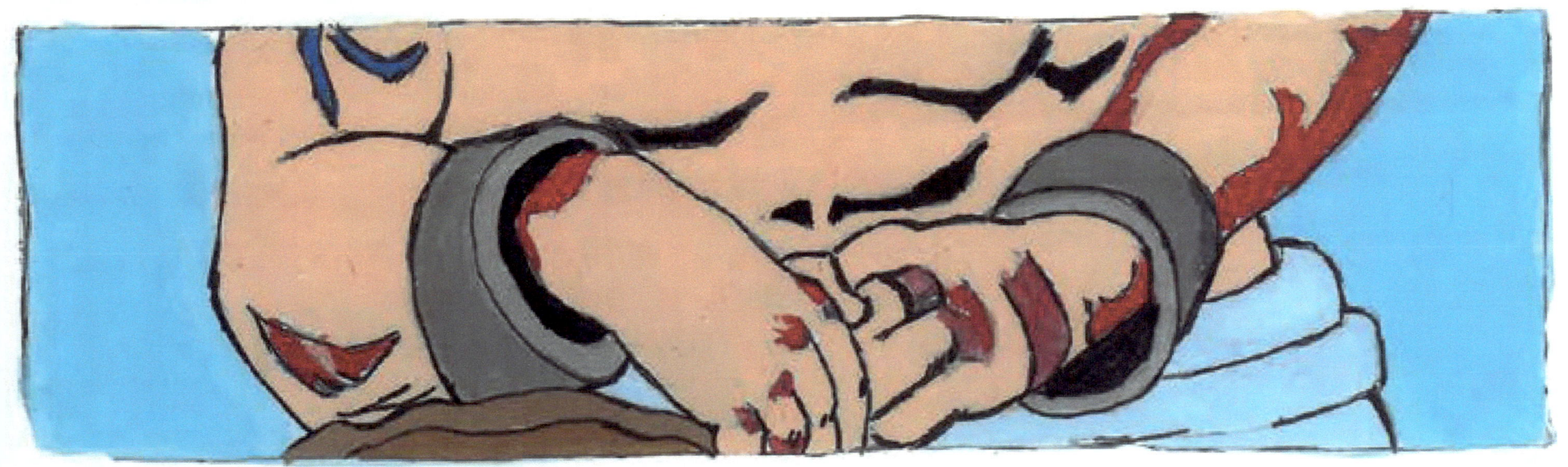

41

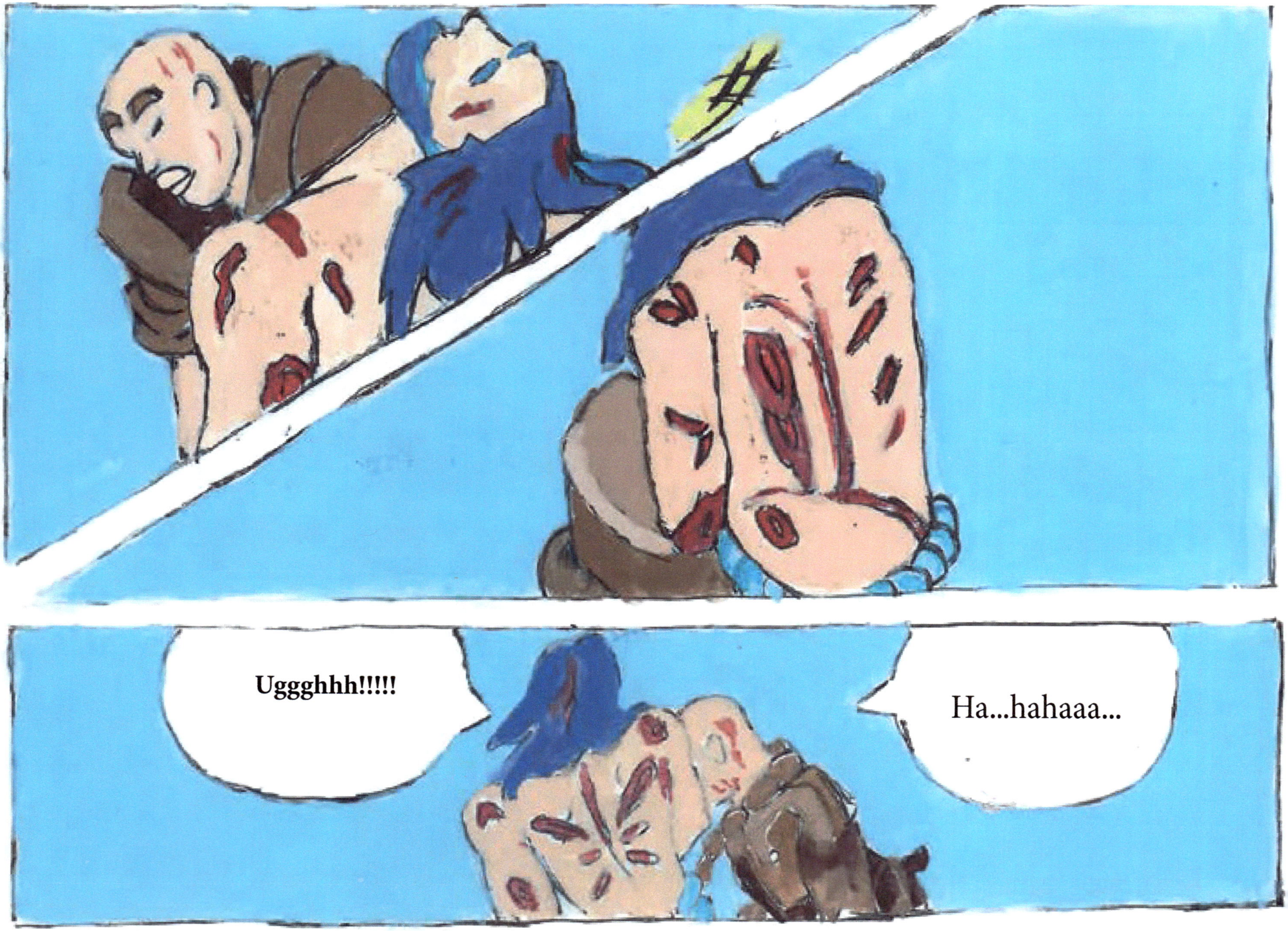

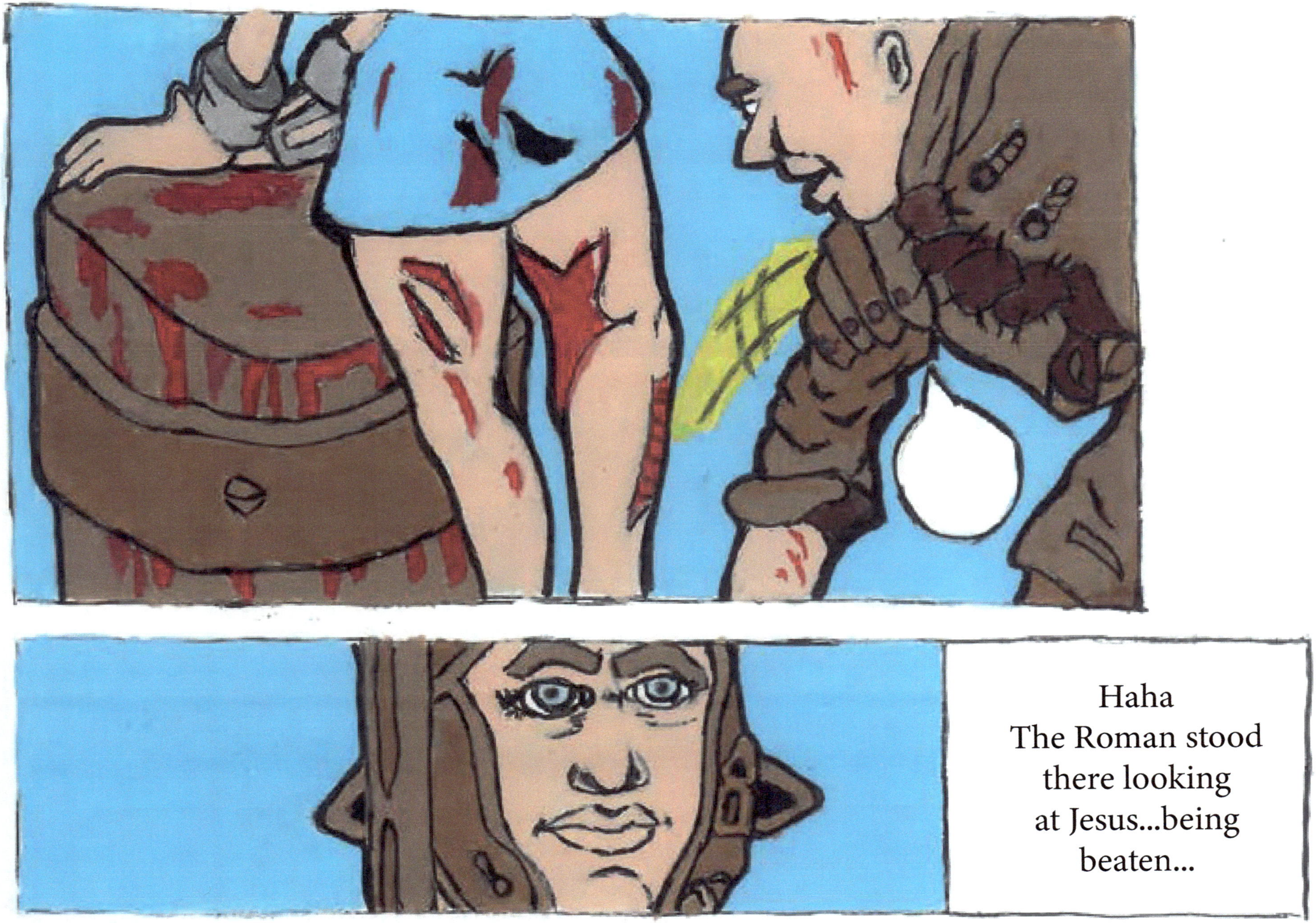

Haha
The Roman stood
there looking
at Jesus...being
beaten...

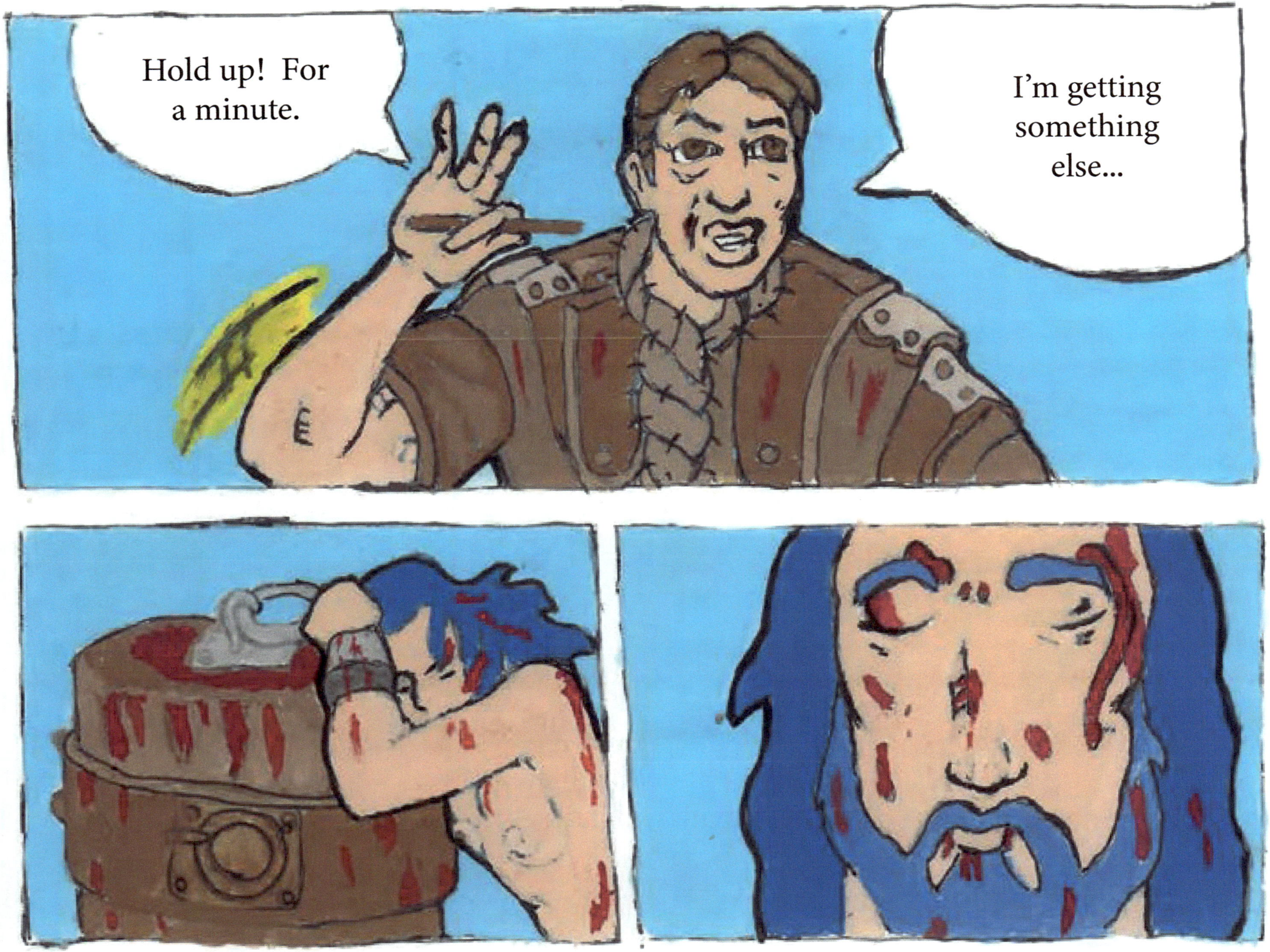
Hold up! For a minute.
I'm getting something else...

Yes

Like this!

Mary put her hand over her mouth with tears in her eyes... as she looked...

Look at this. Do you... really want this...

47

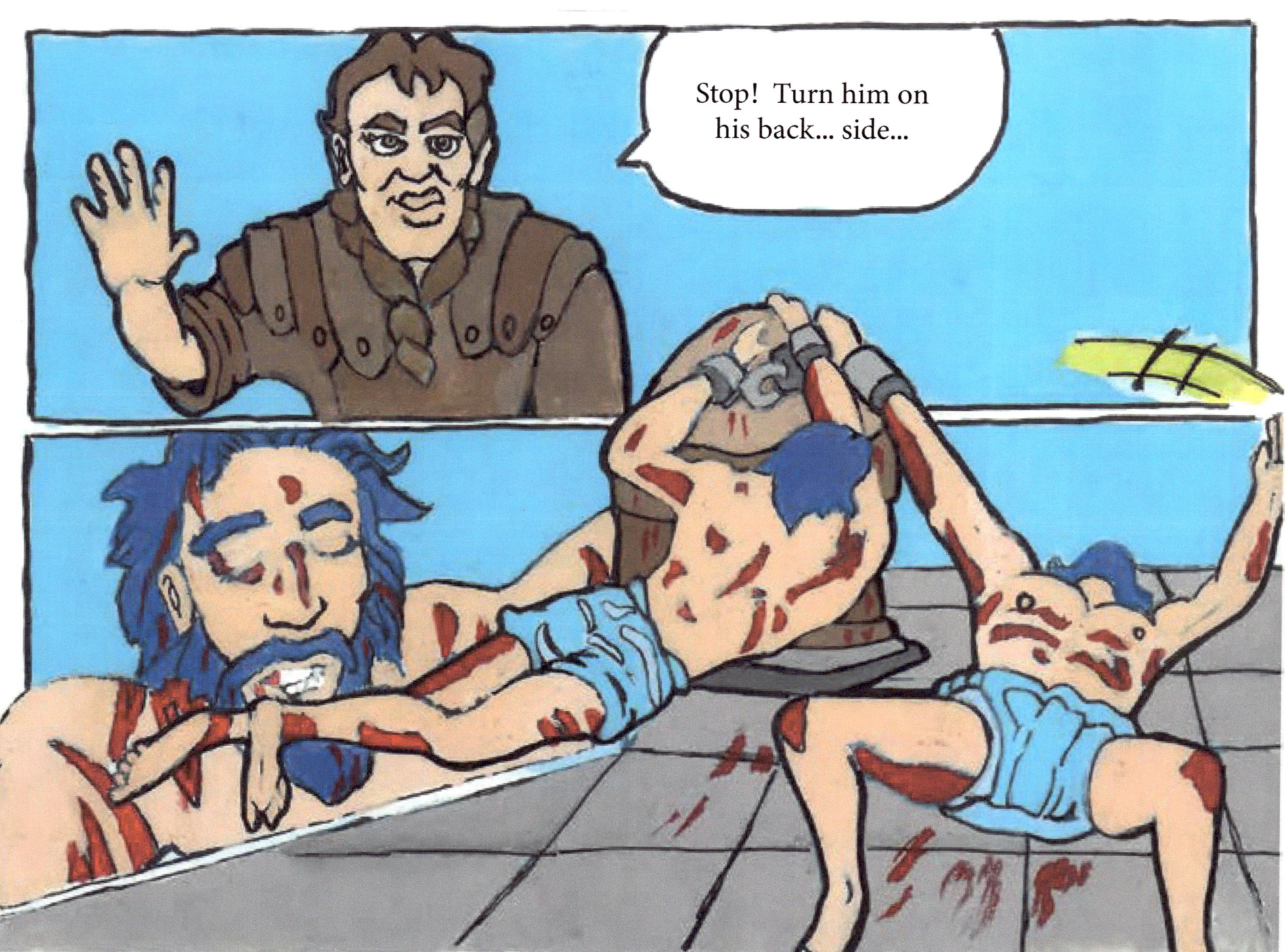

48

49

BLOOD OF JESUS

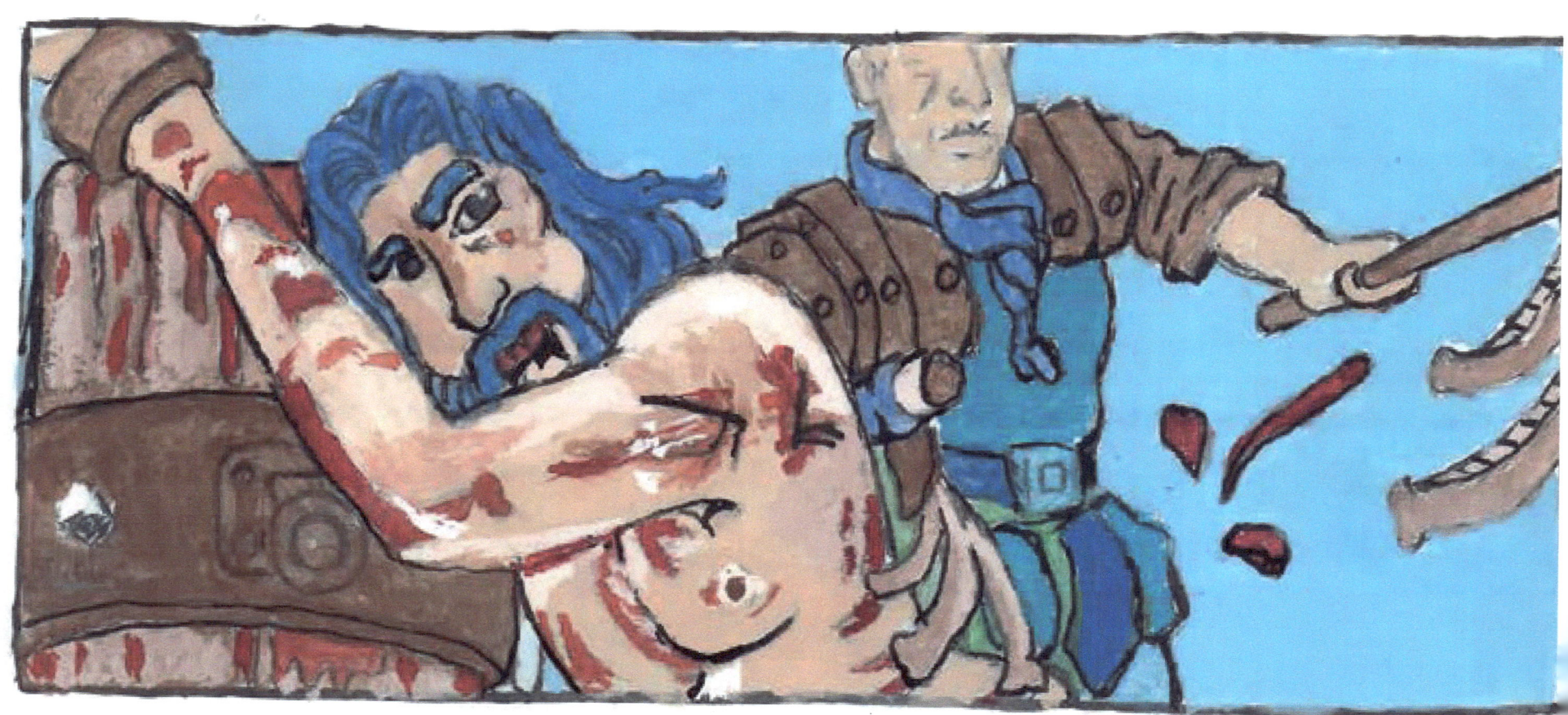

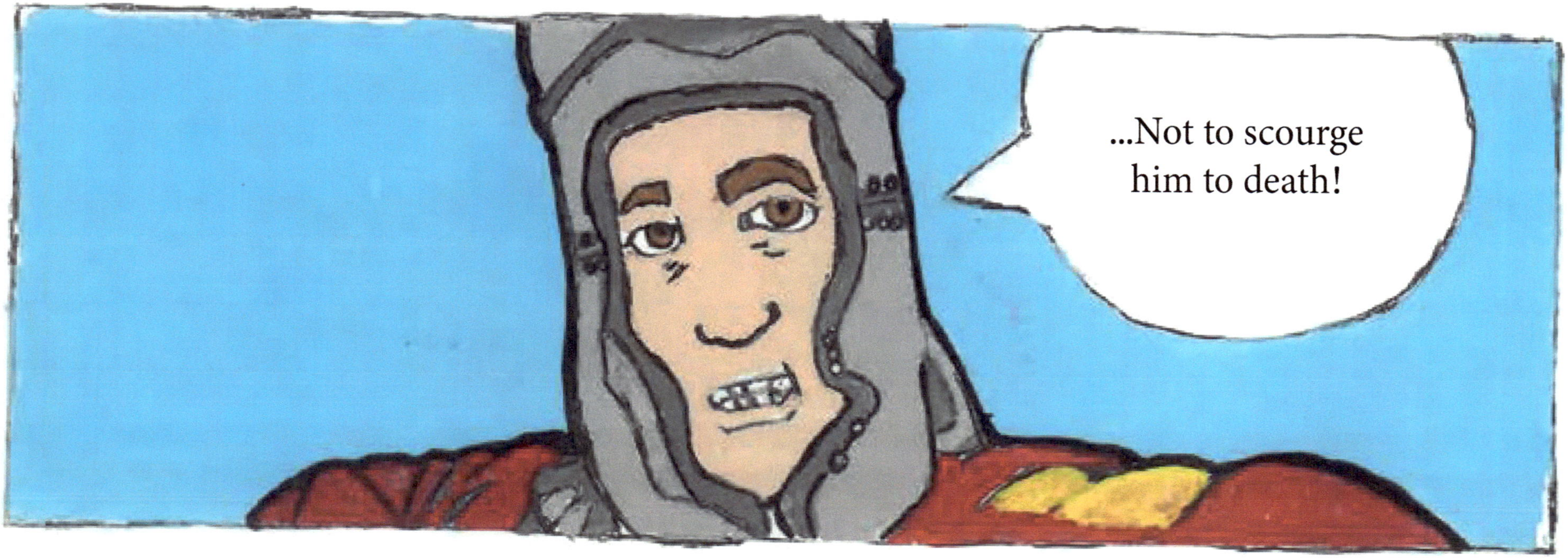
...Not to scourge him to death!

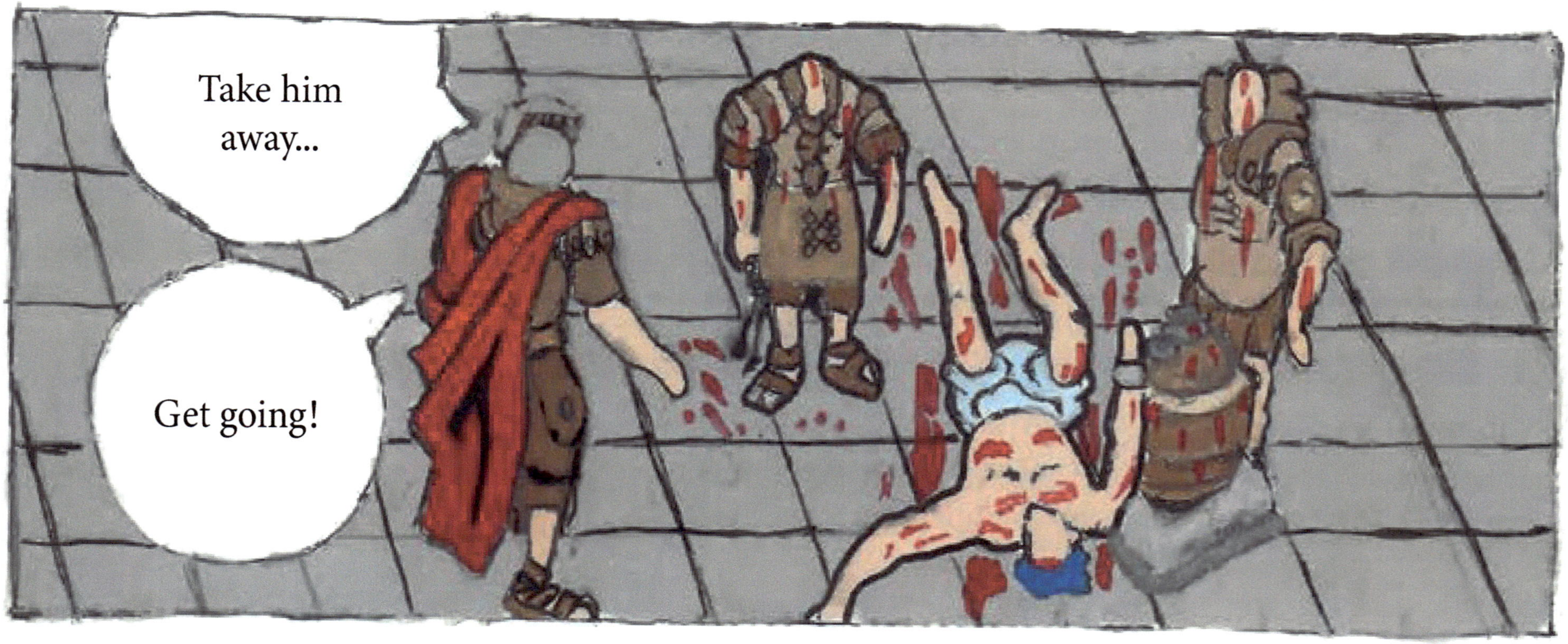
Take him away...
Get going!

52

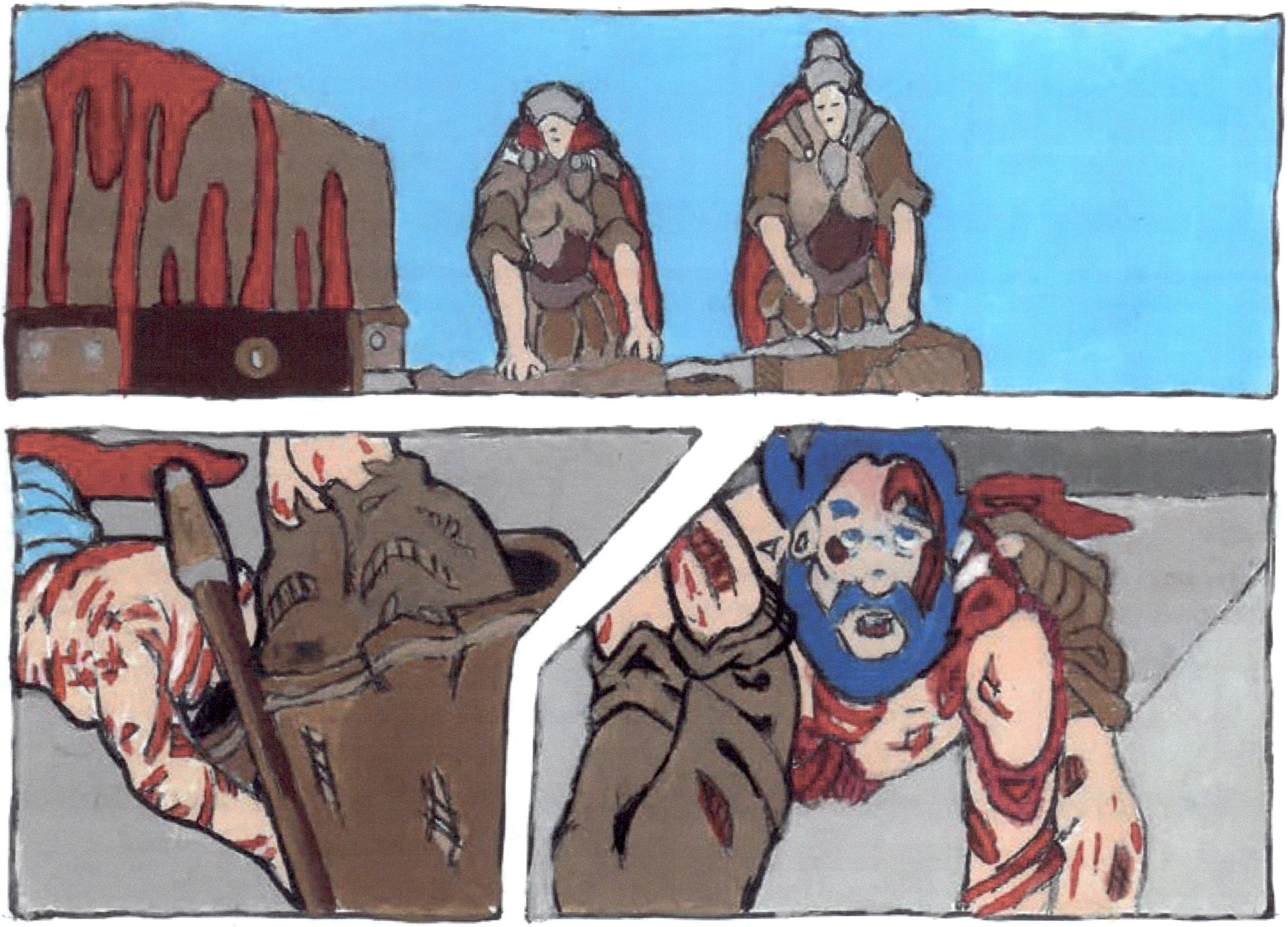

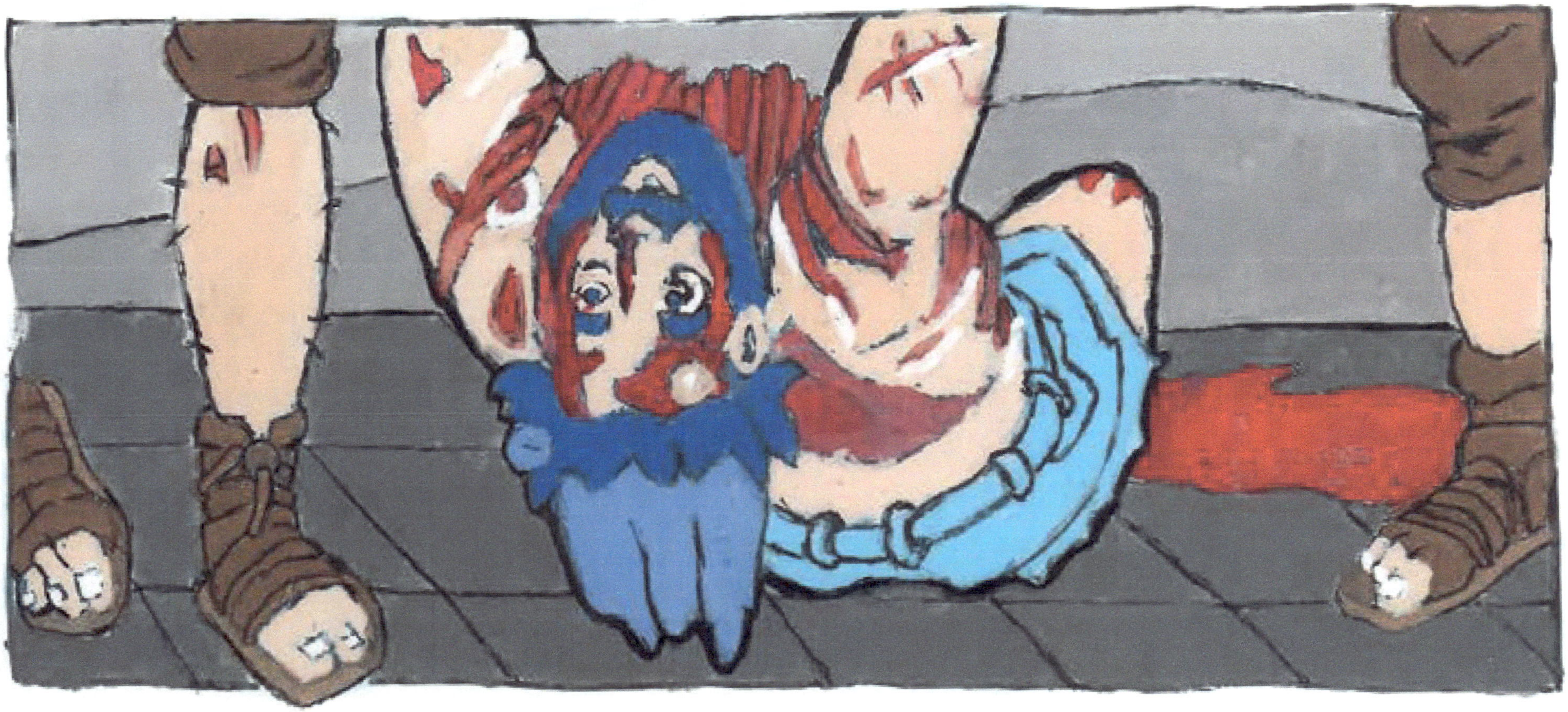

54

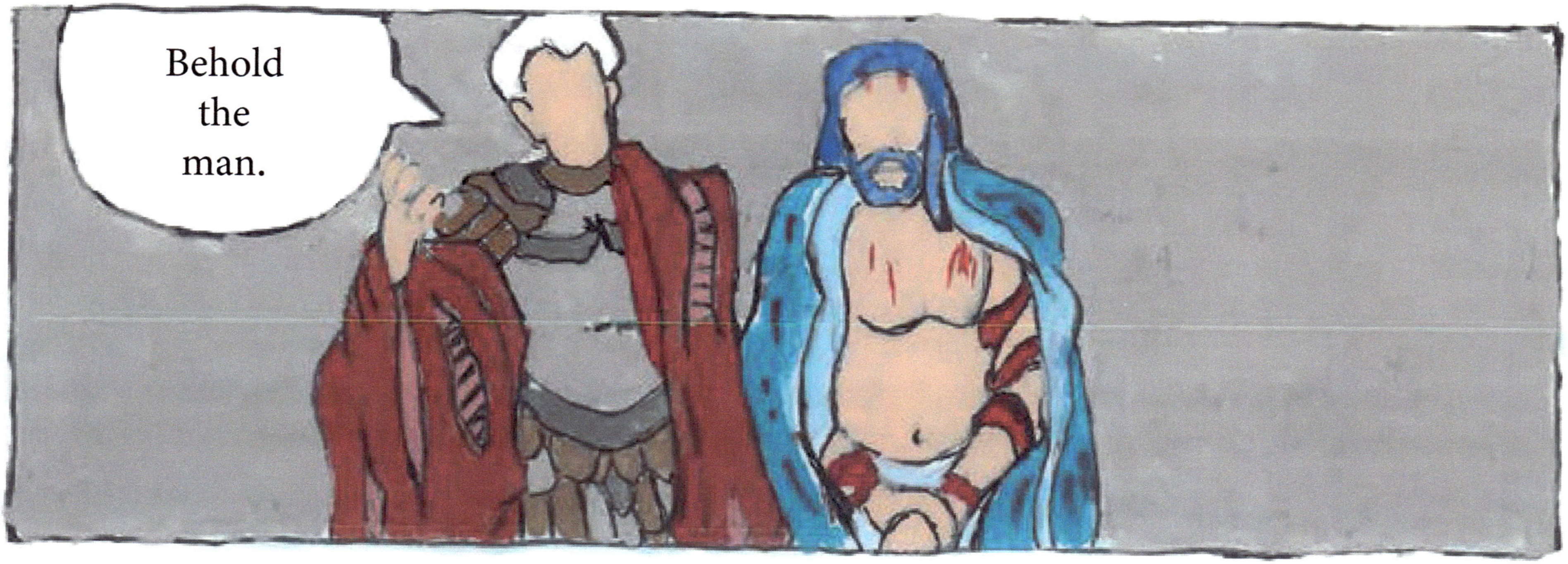
Behold the man.

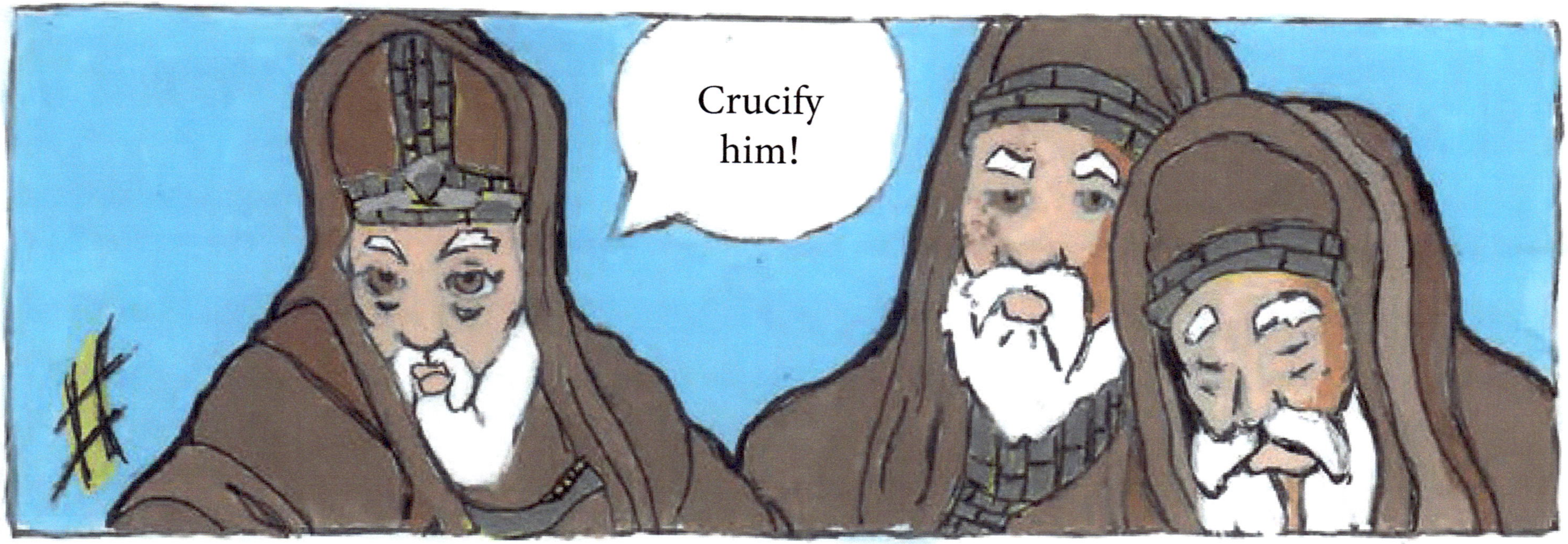
Crucify him!

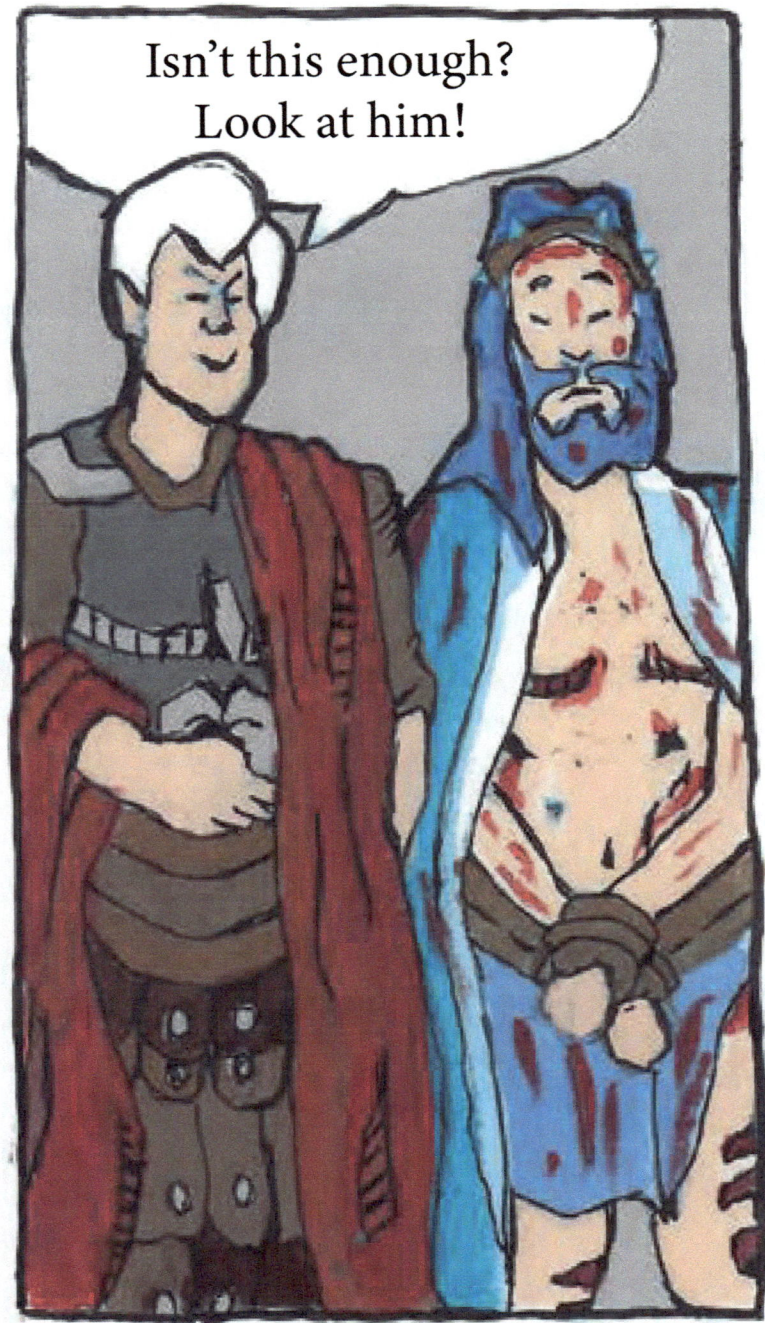

62

64

You have no power over me...
...Except what is given you from above.

Therefore it is he who delivered me to you...
...who has the greater sin.

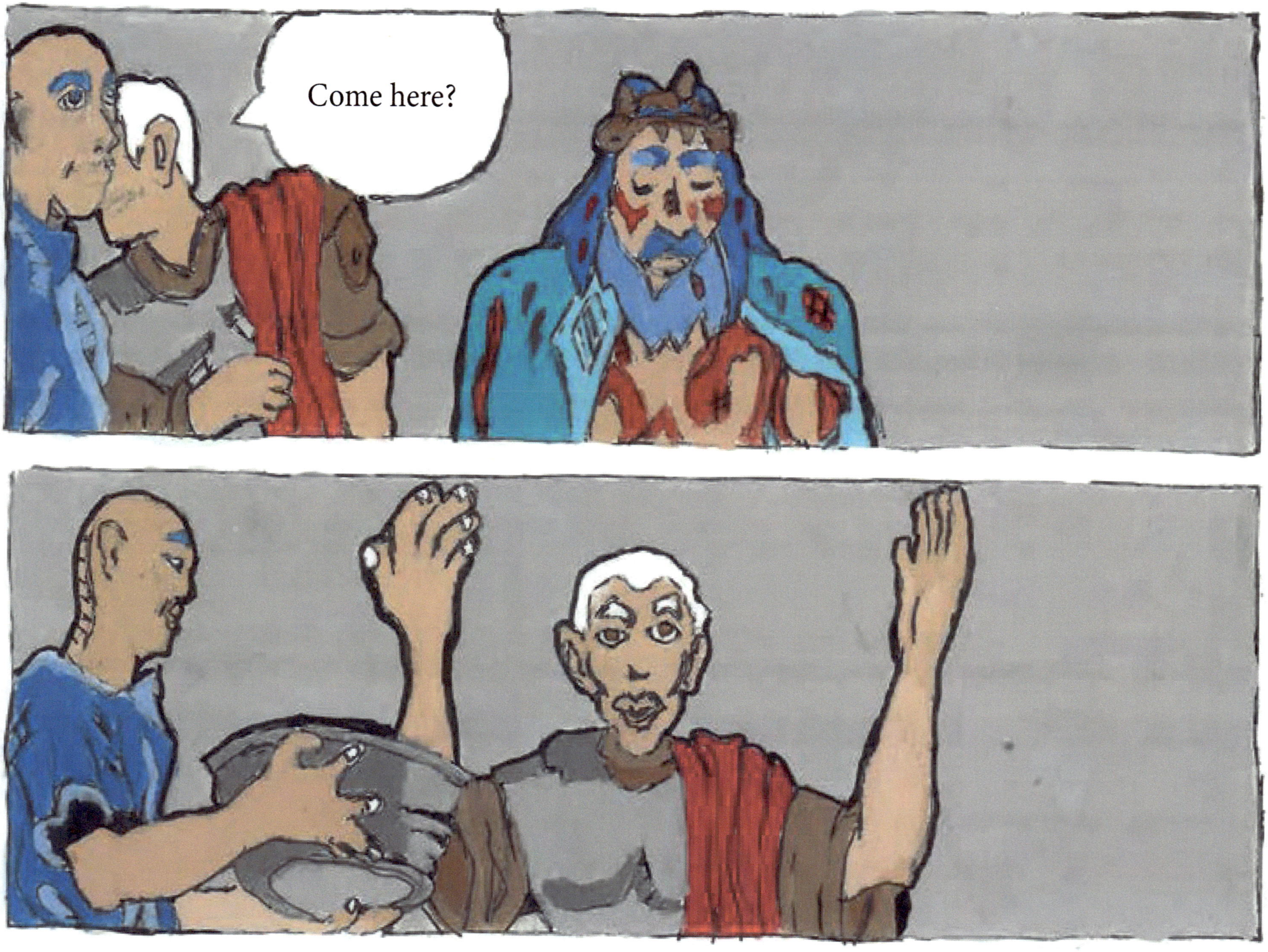
Come here?

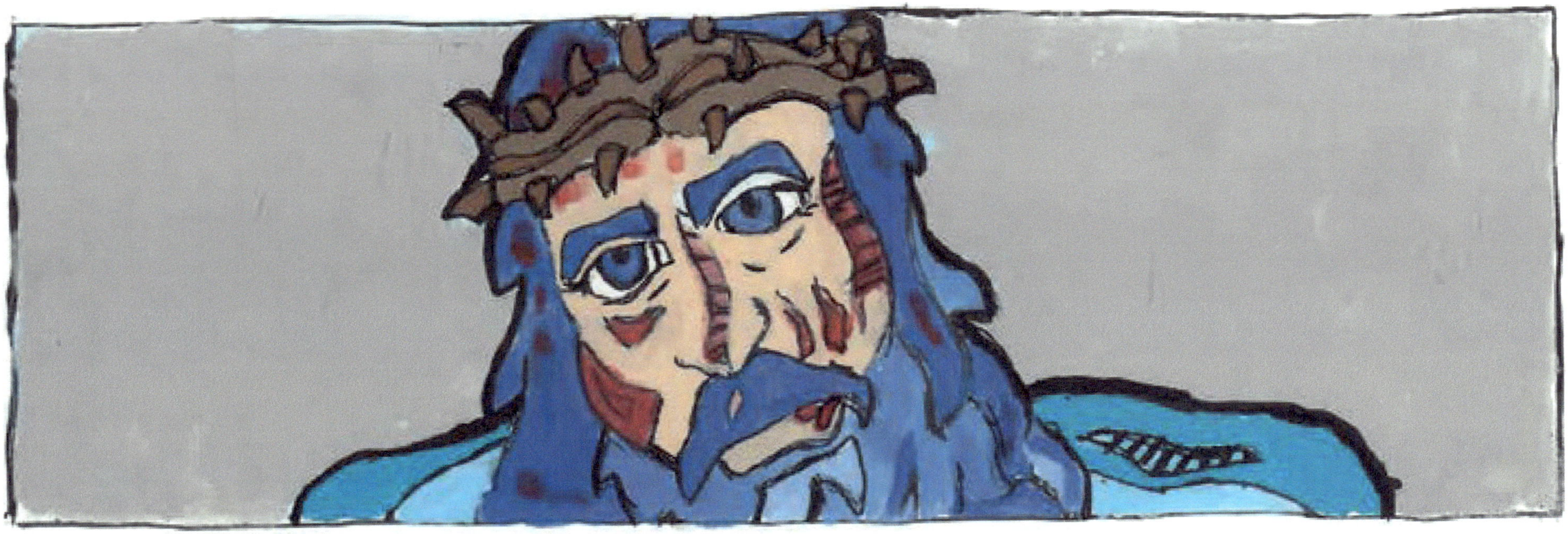

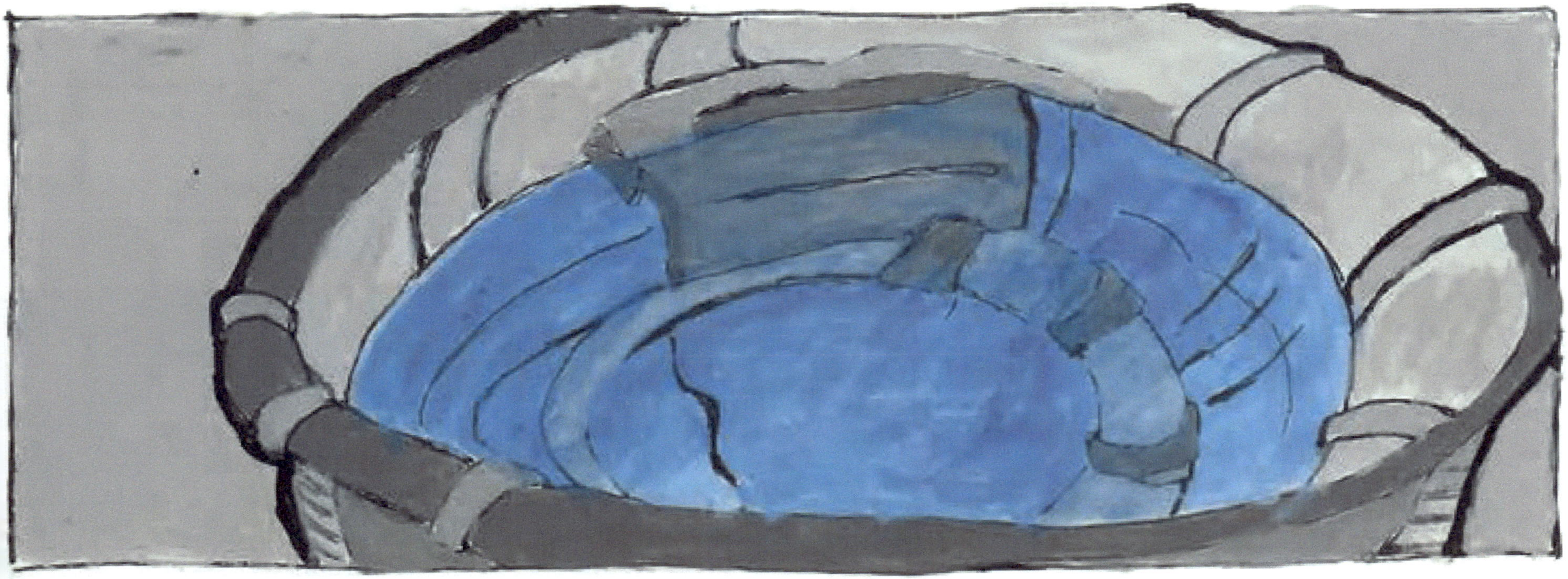

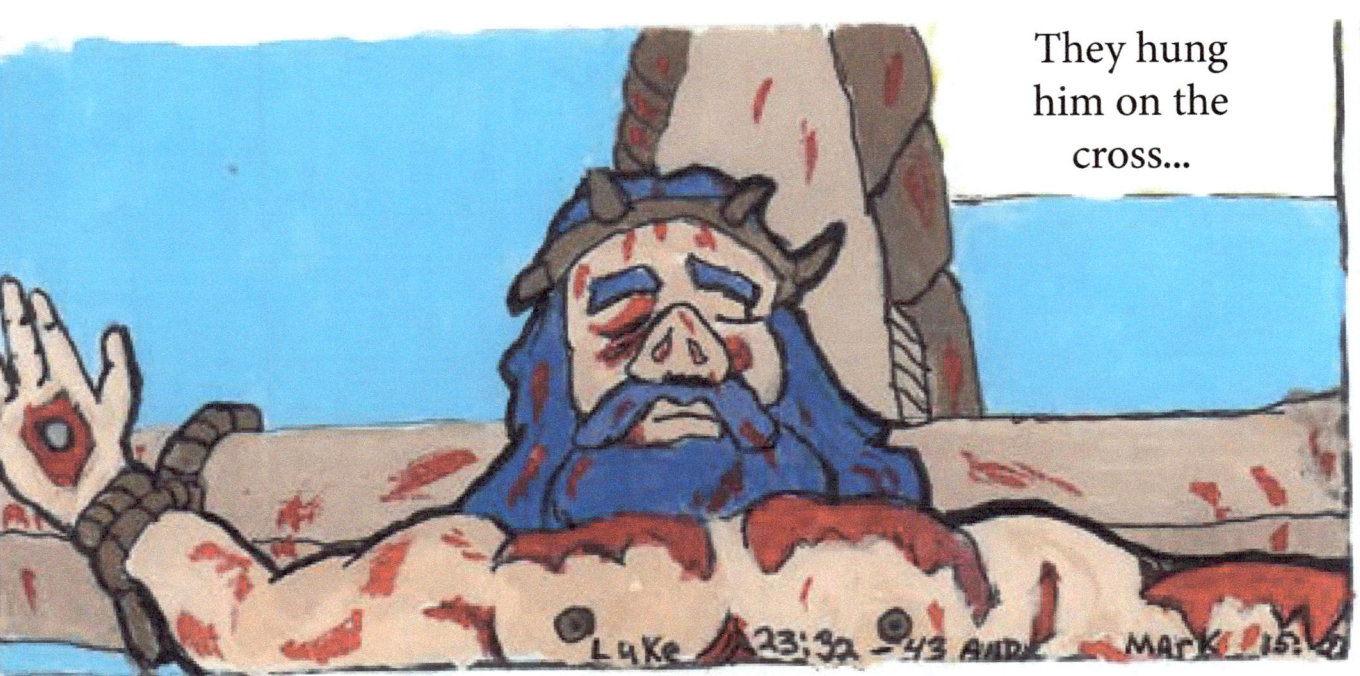

70

71

Father forgive them
They know not what they do...

It is accomplished

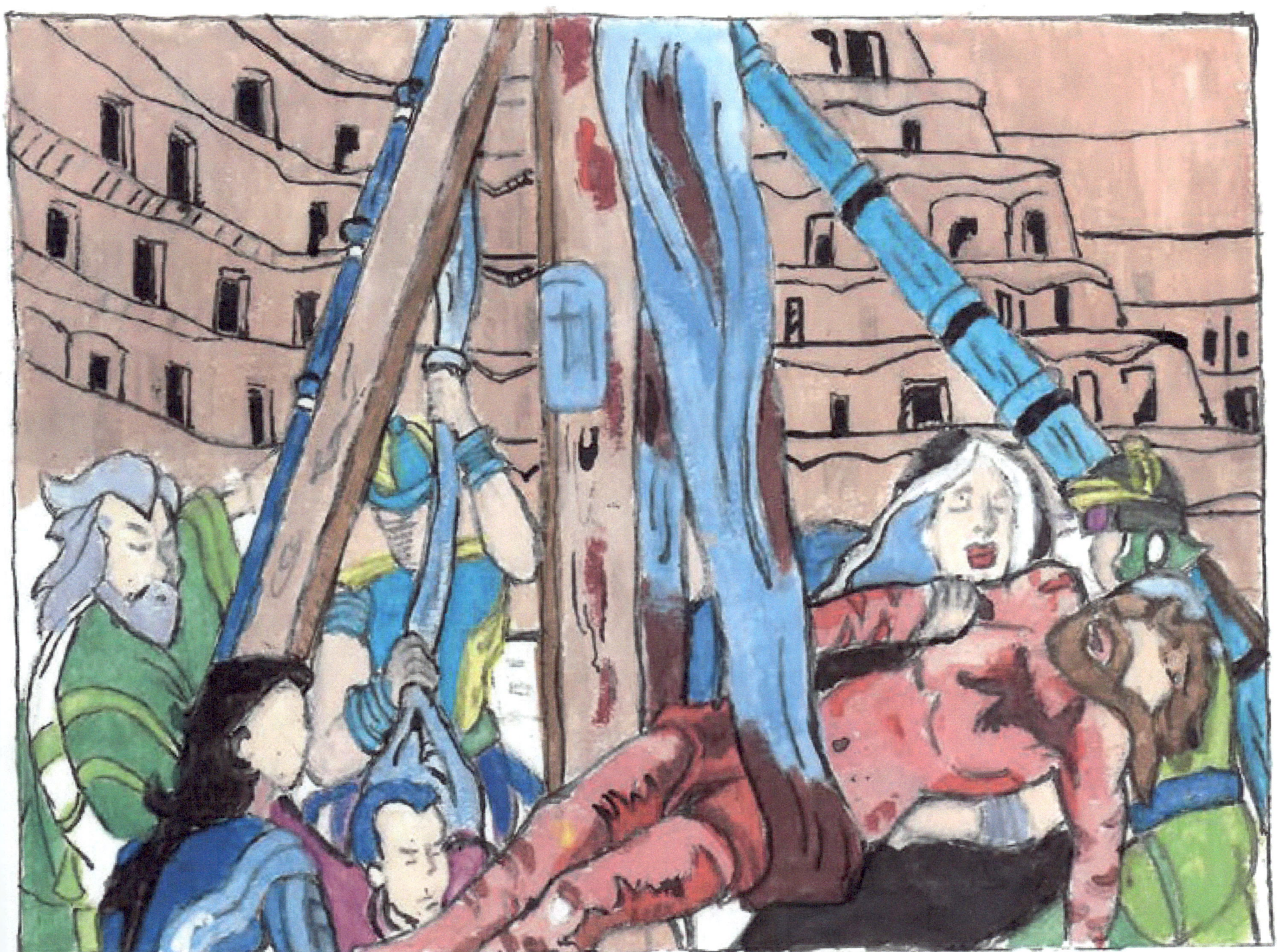

74

I worked for 10 years with the Arizona Cardinals. My brother and I also worked with a skating team for 6 years. Most recently, I worked with Darlington South 500 Raceway, helping them become number one;

I was there for a year. I also work at Oil Mill Darling South. I was born in Washington, DC, and when I was six, my father died of a heart attack, and my mother passed away from the flu a year later.

- *Undrey Nicholson*

IN
LOVING MEMORY
OF

Thomas Charles Smith

&

Lillian Smith

God sent Jesus Christ who died on the cross... For our sins... his blood. Was our sins... An through his name we had a second chance..for the after life.

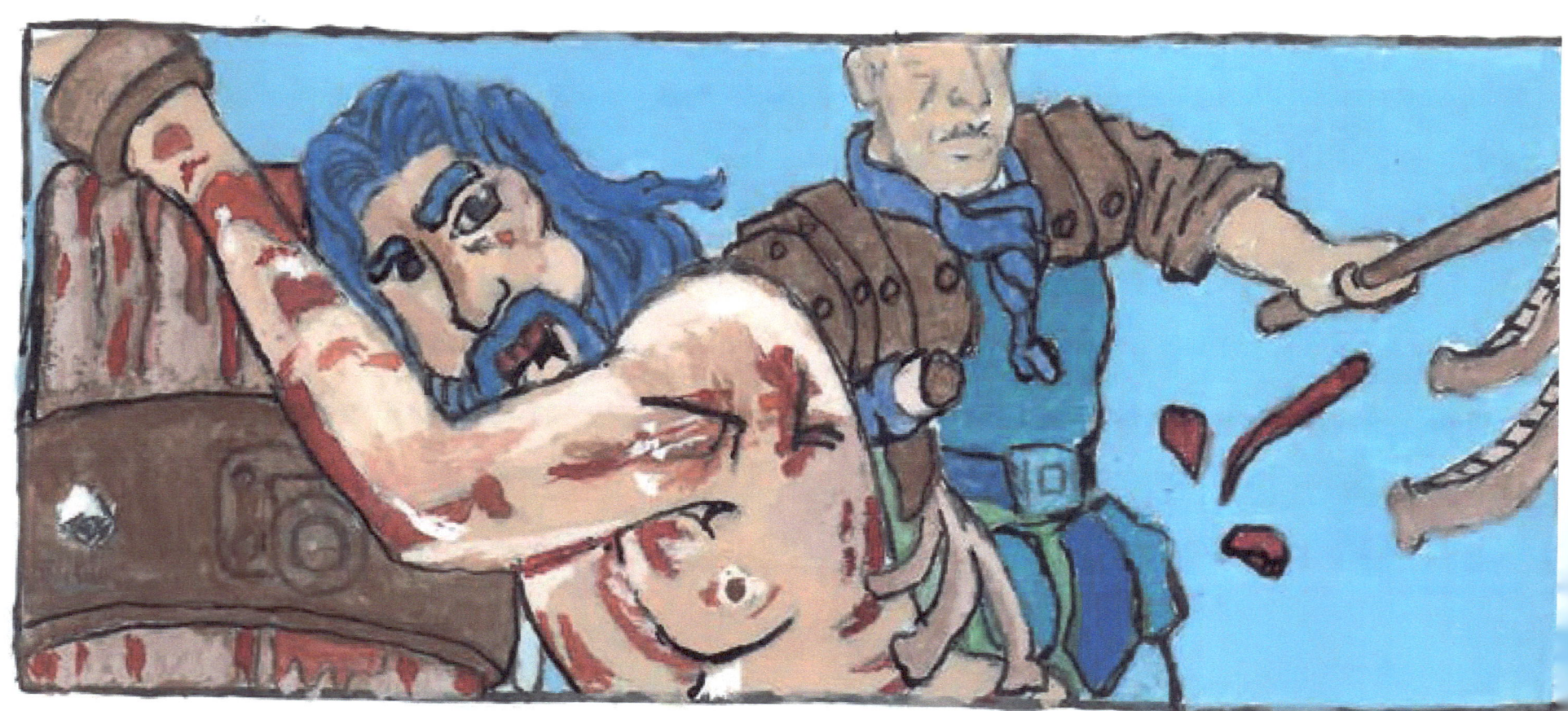

www.ingramcontent.com/pod-product-compliance
Lightning Source LLC
Chambersburg PA
CBHW040813120626

46547CB00004B/530